Step-By-Step Training A Miniature Horse To Drive

Second Edition

Mindy Schroder

www.theessentialhorse.com

Contents Copyright © 2014 by Mindy Schroder

All rights reserved.

Published by Lamplight Press

Web: www.theessentialhorse.com   ~Horse Care, Naturally.

ISBN-13: 978-1494309251

ISBN-10: 1494309254

Cover Image by Mindy Schroder

Photos in book by Mindy Schroder, Loree West and Craig Schroder

ALL RIGHTS RESERVED. No part of this book may be reproduced or transmitted in any form by any means, electronic or mechanical, including photocopying and recording, or by any information storage and retrieval system, except as may be expressly permitted in writing from the publisher. Requests for permission should be addressed to Lamplight Press, Attn: Rights and Permissions, P.O. Box 86, McAllister, MT 59740

This document may be used for informational purposes only.

Dedication

*To all the horses in my life that gave me so much.
I am grateful for all you taught me.*

Contents

Legal Information 6

Acknowledgments 7

The Parts of the Harness.. 10

The Main Parts of a Horse 11

Introduction 13

Chapter One - The Harness 15

Chapter Two - The Vehicles 29

Chapter Three - The Horse 37

Chapter Four - The Groundwork 47

Chapter Five - The Travois 59

Chapter Six - Hitching the Cart 69

The Figure Eight Wrap 79

About The Author 82

Legal Information

Disclaimer of Liability

The author and publishers shall have neither liability nor responsibility to any person(s) or entities with respect to any loss or damage, caused or alleged to be caused directly or indirectly as a result of the information contained in this book, or appearing on The Essential Horse website. While this book is as accurate as the author can make it, there may be unintentional errors, omissions and inaccuracies.

Terms and Conditions

This book is for informational and educational purposes only. The information presented and contained within this book is based on the training and experience of the author. It's content is not intended to be used as a substitute for professional guidance.

Acknowledgements

I want to thank both my husband and my little boy. They were both so very helpful in putting this book together. My husband learned to drive a horse while helping me with these photos!

I would also like to thank the miniature horse mare, Ellie, who was my most brilliant model for most of the photographs in this book. Ellie is worth her weight in gold, she was so patient with me, my husband and my son!

The Parts of the Harness

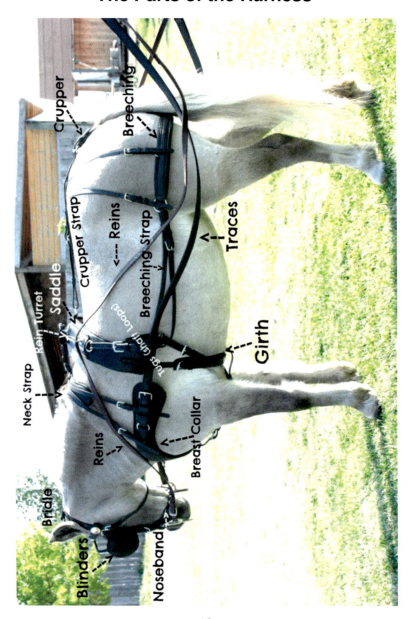

The Main Parts of the Horse

Introduction

I am writing this book to help the beginner driver. It will include many photos as I believe a picture is worth a thousand words, and at times will explain something better than words can. I will explain the parts of the harness and what they do, as well as the parts of the horse. I will go through the steps I take to train a horse to drive, step by step, explaining how to harness a horse, through hitching to a vehicle. It will be a fun read and will help simplify the whole process.

One thing to keep in mind when reading this book is that it is a guide book only. It gives you information about how I train and harness. There are many ways to do this successfully. This is just a guideline. As in life nothing is set in stone and things can change over time. Your horse will grow, mature, gain muscle as you drive and you'll have to adjust your harness to accommodate that. Also harnessing can change with the vehicle you are using.

Driving your horse is a very rewarding experience and a way to bring you closer to your animal. If done correctly both you and your horse will enjoy many years together!

Chapter One
The Harness

"Sometimes the questions are complicated, but the answers are simple."

~Unknown

The harness has three jobs: pulling, stopping and controlling the horse and vehicle.

The most important thing to remember is to spend the extra money and get a quality, well made harness. Those great "deals" on eBay are NEVER a good idea. You should avoid them at all costs. We would have spent less if we had stopped looking for the "best" deal! American or English bridle leather are the best quality leather and worth the money. A well-made harness will cost anywhere between $250 and $1500.

The Bridle

The bridle is much like a riding bridle with the addition of the blinders, the check rein and a noseband. The over check or side check is used to get the horse's head up. This is, unfortunately, a necessary piece of equipment if you are going to be showing AMHR (American Miniature Horse Registry) or AMHA (American Miniature Horse Association) as it is required by both breed associations. When showing in American Driving Society events such as pleasure shows or CDE's (Combined Driving Events), check reins are not allowed.

I find that most horses don't mind the side check but can be annoyed by the overcheck rein. I use a side check and adjust it quite loosely. I do this only when I'm showing my horses in the show ring. Around the farm I don't use a check rein at all. This attachment is a controversial piece of equipment and has started many heated conversations. Everyone seems to have strong opinions on this and most are not afraid to state them! I would recommend that if you are new to driving **leave off the check until you learn more and get hands on help from a trainer.**

Step-By-Step Guide To Training A Miniature Horse To Drive

Step-By-Step Guide To Training A Miniature Horse To Drive

Photo Opposite Left: The side check is the piece of leather that runs from the bit, down the horse's neck and hooks on the waterhook of the saddle.

Photo Left: This shows the overcheck and how it criss crosses the horse's face. It then runs down the neck and hooks to the saddle.

Photo Right: This is a side check adjusted loosely. I recommend you start your horse without using a check rein. The rest of the pictures will show this mare without a check rein.

The blinders are to help the horse pay attention to the job in front of him. It's very important that the blinders fit the horse properly. They should have enough room so the eyelashes don't touch or rub on the inside of the blinder.

The blinders should be adjusted so the horse can still see ahead and to the side, but not behind. If there is a gap between the blinder and the side of the horse's face then the bridle is not adjusted properly. The blinders should be adjusted so the horse's eye is in the middle when seen from the front.

In these photos the bridle is laying flat against these mare's faces, making the blinders effective. They are also adjusted so the eye is in the middle of the blinder.

Photo Opposite Right: Some horses are more comfortable driving without blinders. This is called an open bridle. I found a few of the donkeys I drove preferred to be able to see all around them when driving. This photo is of our Haflinger mare, Marley, who was much more comfortable being able to see everything around her as well.

Step-By-Step Guide To Training A Miniature Horse To Drive

The Breast Collar

The breast collar and traces are how the horse pulls the vehicle. The traces are the part of the harness that attaches to the cart. The horse will lean into the traces and the breast collar when pulling. There are two ways breast collars are made. They are either stitched to the traces, or have a buckle end that allows for more adjustability when harnessing your horse to the cart.

Some breast collars are shaped in a "V". These are the most comfortable for long distance driving and driving over rough ground, such as the cross country course in a Combined Driving Event (CDE).

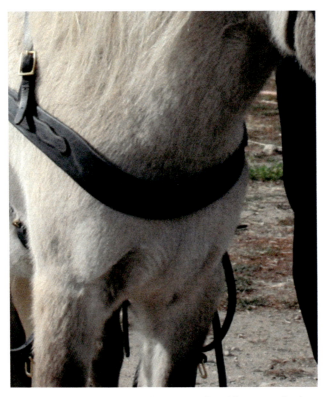

Most harnesses come with this style of breast collar. You want the breast collar to be nice and wide to make the job of pulling you and the cart more comfortable.

Step-By-Step Guide To Training A Miniature Horse To Drive

This is the Freedom Collar made by Camptown Harness. This harness is their Miniature Horse Sport Harness.

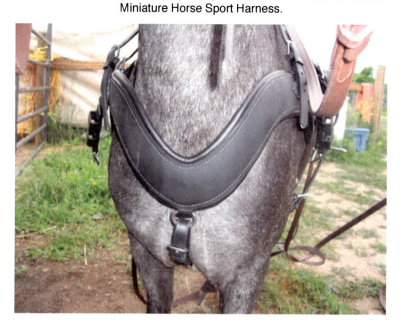

This photo shows how the breast collar hooks to the waterhook on the saddle. This helps stabilize the harness when galloping across country, crossing water, and racing over bumps.

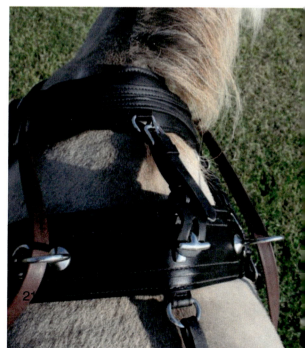

Step-By-Step Guide To Training A Miniature Horse To Drive

Above: A photo of a stitched trace.

Below: Photos of buckle back traces.

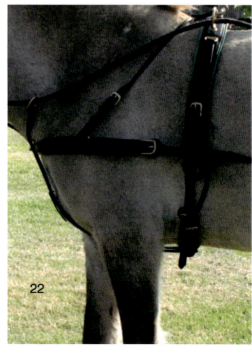

The Saddle

The saddle sits on the horse's back about a hands width back from the shoulder. The saddle has the tugs, the wrap straps and the cinch. It also has the attachment that goes back to the crupper.

The saddle should be well padded for added comfort. I prefer a saddle with a tree as it will allow for more air flow and will fit the horse more comfortably. If your saddle does not have a tree, be sure you have sufficient padding.

Photo Left: Here is another photo of the Camptown Sport Harness. This saddle has a tree that sits up nice and high allowing for good air flow along the horse's spine. It is also nice and wide down the sides and wraps around the horse. When I am driving I do use a pad under this saddle.

Photo Right: This saddle is a little short along the sides of the horse. It requires padding to be comfortable. Because it doesn't have a tree it may press down on the horse's spine and cause some discomfort. Be sure to always use sufficient padding with this kind of saddle.

Step-By-Step Guide To Training A Miniature Horse To Drive

The tugs are the loops which hold the shafts on the harness. They hold the cart on the horse. You can help balance the cart depending on how you set the tugs.

Photo Right: Here you can see the shafts going through the tugs (or shaft loops).

Below: You can see the shafts going through the tugs in this photo as well.

Wrap Straps

Wrap straps or over girths are there to firmly connect the cart to the horse. They are attached to the bellyband and wrap around the shafts. I have two different kinds of straps shown here. One is longer and wraps around the shafts in a figure eight style wrap. The other is an open tug. It has a piece of leather that dangles from the tug and buckles into the over girth, there is no wrapping involved with this one at all.

Photo Left: This is the Figure Eight Wrap. See page 79 for instruction on the Figure Eight Wrap.

Photo Right: The photo shows the buckle down tug. No wrapping, just pull straight down and buckle to the belly band. This set up allows for some float in the shafts which can be good if you are driving across rough country or down bumpy roads.

The Crupper

The crupper is there to help keep the saddle straight. It provides support and prevents the saddle from pressing forward into the withers when braking or going downhill.

When you are adjusting your harness it's important to be as accurate as you can, matching the same number of holes on each side. If your crupper is buckled on the second hole on the left side, buckle it on the second hole on the right side as well. If your belly band is buckled on the third hole on the right side, buckle it as close as you can to the third hole on the left side. The same goes for the buckles on the neck strap and the breeching. This will help keep everything balanced and comfortable for your horse.

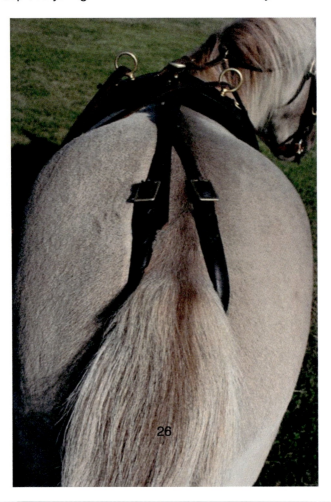

The Breeching

The breeching is there to keep the cart from running over the horse when going down hills. It also aids the horse when backing. They can push against the breeching to push the cart backwards. If your horse stops suddenly and doesn't have a breeching you run the risk of having the cart run up and bump them in the rear. This can be very startling. Breeching is very important to keeping yourself and your horse safe when driving.

If the breeching is adjusted too high it will hurt the underside of the horse's tail and can make it more difficult for the horse to slow the cart down when going downhill. This can cause the horse to be upset. If the breeching is too low it can sweep the horse's feet out from underneath him when going down hill or stopping suddenly.

Photo Right: This breeching is adjusted incorrectly. It's too high up under her tail.

Below: This breeching is adjusted correctly.

A quick overview of the harness: The saddle is the anchor of the whole system, with the tugs holding the cart up, the over girth holding the cart down, the traces pulling it forward, and the breeching holding it back. The art of harnessing is finding a balance between each of those forces so the horse has a comfortable space to work within the harness.

Chapter Two
The Vehicles

"A true horseman does not look at the horse with his eyes. He looks at his horse with his heart."
~Unknown

There are many different styles of carts. I will show photos of a few I like. It is important that the cart be really well balanced. These little guys need all the help they can get! A well-balanced cart will allow your horse to travel a lot further.

A good way to tell if your cart is balanced is to have a friend sit in your cart while you hold the shafts. Hold the shafts at the height they will be on the horse and you'll be able to feel how much weight will be on the horse's back. You don't want more than 5 pounds on the horse's spine. You definitely don't want the horse to carry you as well as pull you!

A perfectly balanced cart should also be able to balance perfectly with a driver in the seat and no one holding the shafts. (I don't recommend trying this without someone standing there ready to grab the shafts just in case!) If the cart isn't balanced in most cases you can adjust this by moving the seat forward or back.

You don't want too much weight pulling upward on the horse's belly either. This can happen if the tugs are adjusted too short, or if the seat is too far back. The weight of the driver will cause the ends of the shafts to press upward which can make the horse feel like it is being lifted off the ground. That isn't balanced either. It's important to play with it until it is balanced. If you can't get it to balance, then get rid of it and buy a different cart. Balance is key to having an enjoyable driving experience with your horse.

The Easy Entry Cart

This cart is a great training cart. The Easy Entry Cart is generally inexpensive. Most people like it because, as the name suggests, it is very easy to get into and out of. They come in metal, wood and a combination of both. They are adjustable for many different sizes of horses from 30" all the way up to 38".

We really love the light wooden carts built by the Amish. They have lovely big wheels which make pulling the cart easier for the horse. The bigger the wheels the easier it will roll along. I prefer big wheels when I drive the smaller miniature horses.

These carts have adjustable seats. The seats are bolted to the floors and with just a crescent wrench you can loosen those bolts, slide the seat forward or back, depending on how it needs to be adjusted and then tighten the bolts back up.

The easy entry carts also have a single tree. The single tree swings gently with the movement of the horse's shoulders as it moves along in the shafts. The single tree is an important part of the cart as it will help the horse do it's job in comfort.

Step-By-Step Guide To Training A Miniature Horse To Drive

Above: A close up of the metal easy entry and the wooden single tree. If your cart does not have a single tree you can order one through any cart maker and attach it to your cart. I prefer the wooden single trees. The cart above did not have one, so I ordered this one and attached it myself.

Below: An Amish built cart with the lovely big wheels.

The Roadster/Sulky/Hyperbike

These carts are relatively inexpensive, lightweight and easy for the miniature horse to pull. They are really fun carts that make you feel like you are flying!

The hyperbikes are easy to take apart and put together making them the perfect cart for putting in the tack room of your horse trailer and heading to the beach with your miniature horse. If you are lucky enough to live by a beach!

The hyperbike was built to have low drag and the frame helps absorb the shock which means it's lightweight, easy to pull and less shock is transmitted to the horse when pulling. I think this is why my miniature horses love pulling it.

The shafts go from the horse all the way around to the back of the seat which can make getting in and out a bit of a challenge. The key is to have your horse well trained so it stands quietly while you sit on the seat and then swing your legs over the shafts. The hyperbike has stirrups mounted to the outside of the shaft that your feet sit in. The sulky or roadster has stirrups mounted to the inside of the shafts so you swing your legs to the inside of the shafts, then set your feet in the stirrups.

You can use the hyperbike in CDE's (Combined Driving Events) cross country courses. The roadsters and sulkies can be driven in the AMHR/AMHA classes.

Below is a photo of the hyperbike. I love the seat with the back on it!

The stirrups are attached to the outside of the shafts.

Above: The hyperbike hitched to my mare. In this photo you can see how close the cart is to the horse. It makes you feel like you are riding your miniature!

The Show Cart

Show carts are expensive but beautiful. If you plan on really getting into show driving either in CDE's or the AMHR/AMHA shows, then I highly recommend that you have a nice show cart.

They usually have a wooden basket that can be covered with a vinyl or patent boot. Sometimes the baskets are removable turning your show cart into a roadster. If you take the boot off and leave the basket on then you have a country cart.

Show carts sit down low to the ground. The shafts start at the horse and go all the way back to the seat making it necessary that your horse be patient while you climb over the side to get in. Don't stand with all your weight in the basket as they are not made for that, but simply put your leg over the side and slide onto the seat.

These carts really help your horse strut his stuff in the show ring. You both will look classy and professional when you show up in this rig!

The Buggy/Phaeton

The buggy/phaeton has four wheels making it a more stable and secure vehicle. I always loved my buggy! All my horses loved pulling it as all the weight of the vehicle sits on the ground and doesn't balance on the shafts at all. This makes it much easier for the horse to pull.

Some buggies are made out of wood and some made out of metal. Typically the four wheeled vehicles used for CDE's are made out of metal as they are safer to gallop across country in. Buggies are customizable to either a single horse or a two-up or four-up team. You can show in these vehicles and they are wonderful for parades!

Chapter Three
The Horse

"If a horse becomes more beautiful in the course of it's work, it is a sign that the training principles are correct."
~ Colonel Podhajsky

Lets discuss the conformation of the driving horse. A horse with a nice laid back shoulder will have a longer gait and will be able to cover more ground than a horse with a straighter shoulder. Horses with a straighter shoulder have a place as well. They have a more upright gait which can be very animated. They don't cover as much ground in a stride, but are also fun to drive.

A horse with a longer back can have less stamina than a horse with a short back. If the horse has a long back and shorter legs, it is harder for them to stride out comfortably for a long drive. Often times horses with a longer back, if not trained properly, will get a sore back as well. They must be trained to use their hind end and round their top line, to strengthen the muscles in the back. This is so for every driving horse.

A nice length of neck, most importantly a clean throatlatch, is essential in aiding the horse to properly collect. A horse with a reasonable length of neck, compared to the rest of it's body, will have an easier time carrying the frame for a long period of time. A horse with a heavier throatlatch area will not be able to collect, because the thickness of the throatlatch will inhibit it's breathing when the poll is flexed.

It's important to have a plan when starting a driving horse. Do you want to pleasure drive, compete in breed shows, do CDE's, or maybe parades? Most horses can do a couple of these things, but a show driving horse will be much different than a calm, quiet parade or pleasure horse.

It is also important to look at the conformation of the horse to determine which discipline will best suit them. Keep in mind the size of the horse and the size of the driver. Will your horse be able to pull you long distances easily?

Decide if you want to drive a stallion, gelding, or a mare. There are pluses and minuses to all. Stallions usually can go all day on sheer testosterone, but you have to watch them in a group and in parades.

The mares are fun too, but they have their heat cycles, which can make them harder to deal with at times.

Geldings are steady, true to their work and easier to take care of.

Of course every horse is an individual and should be evaluated as such. There are always exceptions to every rule!

Be sure if you choose to drive a stallion you are aware of certain rules at the places you will be driving. Sometimes they don't allow stallions, because of the problems that can arise.

This mare has a nice clean throat latch area. She is able to round up and be on the bit beautifully.

Step-By-Step Guide To Training A Miniature Horse To Drive

This mare has a short back and long legs which help her naturally use her hind end better. She is not collected as far as being on the bit, but she is driving up from behind nicely. Collection comes from behind, it's not just about having the horse on the bit.

Below: This mare is collected beautifully, on the bit and driving up from behind. She is just floating along!

Now let's compare two driving geldings.

The brown gelding is a 12-year old, 31-inch driving gelding that has been driving for about 5 years. He was a stallion until late in his life.

In this photo you can see he has a bit of a heavier throatlatch, which made it a little more difficult to collect and be able to breathe well. When I showed him and was actively driving him I sweated his neck. This is an extensive process and not something I would recommend for everyone. It requires keeping a close eye on your horse. It does help tighten up that area however.

He has a neck that comes out of the middle of his chest instead of the top. I call this a chest-neck. When they are built this way it's harder for them to lift their front end in an extended trot. Horses that are built this way usually have a steeper shoulder which causes their trotting action to be more up and down. Their front legs have a more up and down motion.

He has a longer back and short legs which means he fits more in a rectangle than a box. You can see in both of these pictures he is butt high. This means it's a bit harder for him to bring his hind end up under his body. You can also see he is well muscled in his hind end, which has happened with careful training and not over doing it with him.

Learn your horse's short comings so you can help strengthen them, developing a happy, healthy driving horse you can enjoy for years.

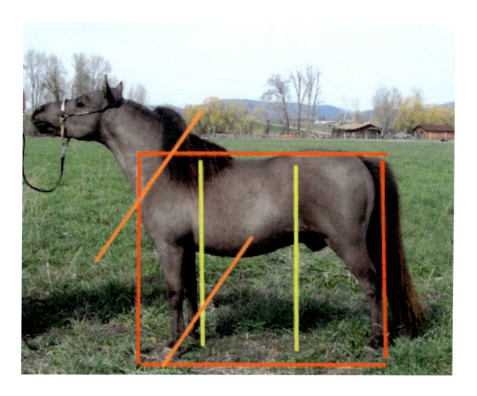

The pinto gelding is a three year old in this picture. He was just beginning his driving career.

He has a higher set neck. You can see in this picture it comes out from his chest a bit higher. This causes his shoulders to be more laid back, creating an opening in his front end that allows him to have more extension with his front end. I call these kinds of horses Daisy Cutters. They can really throw those front feet out, snapping the heads off the daisies.

He has a shorter back and nice, clean long legs. He fits in a box very neatly. When you draw a box on your horse's picture they should measure the same from the ground to the withers as they do from the shoulder to the rump. Then they should measure one-third shoulder, one-third body and one-third hind end.

The angles in both of these pictures show how the shoulder angle matches the angle of the pastern. You can change the angle of the shoulder with the proper gymnastic exercises. Horses don't have a collar bone, the front end is connected to the vertebrae like a big sling. So the entire front end can move forward and back as much as 4 - 6 inches. It's simply amazing what some good training and encouraging good posture can do for your horse.

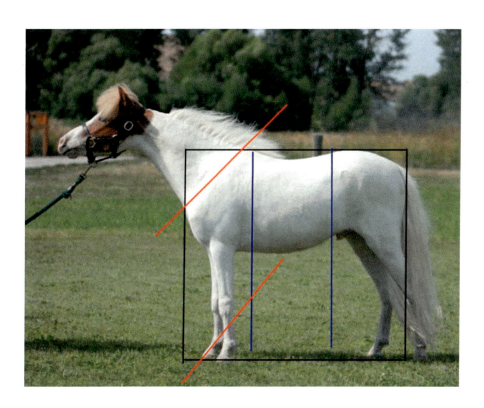

Being able to honestly evaluate your horse will help you know your horse's weaknesses so you can strengthen them. If you pretend he is perfect, you run the risk of hurting him.

This is my horse Billy Blaze, as a yearling. When I got him I was told he had a "ewe" neck, a hammer head and a straight shoulder. I want to add he had a weak back and top line as well.

I knew, from experience, most of what others would call his conformation was actually a posture problem.

Below is the same horse (Billy Blaze) as a three year old. I spent a lot of time teaching him to move with his head down, tightening up his topline and relaxing the muscle under his neck, changing his look from a "ewe" neck to a nice strong neck. In doing this his shoulders also moved back and he lost that extreme straight shoulder.

One exercise I used to help his topline is something I call "Point-to-Point." I simply encouraged him to put his head down and look where he is going.

While we would walk down the road I would put all of my focus and intention on a bunch of grass just up the road from us, about 100 feet ahead of where we were walking. I would focus on the grass and we would walk straight for it. It didn't take long before Billy could feel my intention focus in on the grass bunch and he too would start looking at it as we approached. If he went to the same grass I was looking at he would get to eat it! If he missed and tried for a different bunch of grass, then I would simply encourage him to keep walking by swinging my rope at his belly (I would not pull on his head at all), and we would try again. You can do this on your obstacle course and instead hide cookies all around or play "Point-to-Point" in your pasture.

Essentially what this exercise did was get him to focus downward instead of up in the air or way out on the horizon. This helped his top line build and improved his focus and attention.

You will use focus when you drive. It's amazing how the horse can feel where you are looking and will attempt to drive there. So if you want to avoid the ditch, don't look at it! Look in the direction you want to drive and your horse will head in that direction. Look at your horses ears and you will lose momentum and forward motion.

Focus and body language are very important when training horses.

Chapter Four
The Groundwork

"Develop a lesson plan. The more steps in a process, the less chance you have of slipping up and the faster you'll be able to proceed."

~John Lyons

When I start a driving horse, I spend a lot of time on the ground work. I spend time brushing them and getting to know their sensitive, or sticky, spots. Then I can help the horse through those issues. It's important the horse be comfortable being touched all over it's body. The harness covers a lot of their body and they should feel comfortable when wearing it and working for me. Spending this time with the horse, not demanding anything of it, is a great way to bond and just simply relax.

Ground work is the basis for everything you will do later. Be sure you do lots of ground work, really teaching the horse "Whoa" and to focus on you. This time sets the foundation for the years to come. If you have done your ground work thoroughly and well, your horse will remember it forever.

I spend time teaching them to be confident crossing wooden bridges, tarps, muddy ground, pavement, and gravel. We work on side passing, backing and going over trotting poles in a confident manner. It's important the horse understands the different body language and becomes handy at many different obstacles. I will toss in a jump here and there to keep things interesting during the ground work phase as well.

I lunge them and work on voice commands, walk, trot, canter, WHOA. The whoa command is the most important. I think it's very important for the horse to know and understand this command before I ever hitch them to a travois or a cart. I will start the whoa command with my babies when I am halter training them. They know it by the time I am ready to train for the cart.

Usually I spend a lot of time on the obstacle course and getting the horse familiar with the harness and how it feels to wear it while it's moving around the obstacles. I like to start them in just the halter at first so they are very responsive and focused even without the bit. We spend time ground driving in the halter, through the obstacle course, down the road, around the farm, and through the fields. They must be able to maneuver the obstacle course when ground driving before I put the travois on. The obstacle course will build confidence in your horse.

This is a really fun part of the training. Most horses have just been led through the obstacles and teaching them to drive through keeps them interested and enjoying your training sessions. It helps make it feel more like play than work. My horses meet me at the gate when it's time to work. Remember to keep it fun!

If you start to feel frustrated or angry during your session, just put the horse away until you can get your emotions under control. There is no room for frustration or anger in a training session. Your horse will be happy to do what you ask if you have prepared it well, as long as it understands what you are asking. If it is fighting you, it's most likely confused and you need to slow down, breathe, smile and try again. Breaking your challenge down into smaller more manageable pieces will also help your horse understand what you are asking.

I use lots of praise, such as "Good boy!" and petting during my training sessions. Some horses don't love to be touched, so for those I will just simply wait. Give them a little breather, time to think about what you've just done. Soak time. It's the release that teaches and allowing your horse the time to think about what you've just done will go a long way to having a happy, willing horse tomorrow.

Obstacle Course

Be creative when designing your obstacle course. The more you introduce to your horse now (in a controlled manner) the better off you will both be when you head out on the road, go to horse shows, or drive in parades.

I've driven in some big parades in the city center and there are some interesting things you and your horse will encounter. Bridges, the painted lines on the road, grates, fluttering plastic bags in the road, and kids running out to get candy being thrown off the float in front of you.

If you have prepared your horse and provided a strong foundation, then you won't have any trouble as you head out into the real world. You can enjoy your driving time with your horse, feeling confident, instead of worried and stressed out. Your horse will thank you! The most important thing is to let your imagination go wild. Don't be afraid to try new things and expose your horse to new and different challenges.

Here is a short list of a few things you can use as obstacles:

Pedestal
For this you can use something as simple as a frisbee or a bucket lid on the ground. Even just a block of wood will work. The idea is to get your horse comfortable placing it's feet on an unfamiliar surface. This will build your horse's confidence in you.

Another thing you can do is visit your local tire place and pick up an old, used bobcat tire. I like the bobcat tires because they are a little smaller, but very heavy duty. They easily support the weight of a full grown, big horse. Then you can bolt one or two pieces of 5/8" or 3/4" plywood to one side of the tire using carriage bolts, so there are no sharp edges.

Full sized horse, Billy Blaze, standing on my bobcat tire pedestal. I love this pedestal because I can move it around. I needed something that was portable.

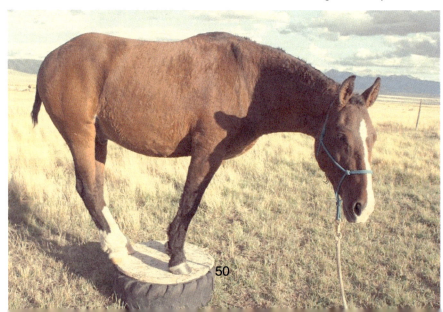

Tarp
Any size or color tarp is appropriate. It's a good idea to use different colors such as orange, blue, silver, brown, black. Every color looks a bit different to your horse. I've found big black garbage bags work great with the miniature horses as well. They are very scary to step on because they look a lot like a big black hole.

Tarps are great for simulating water and unfamiliar surfaces. You can play around with having your horse be comfortable stepping on the tarp as well as wearing it! To help your horse become confident about wearing it, start with the tarp folded up smaller and gradually unfold it and unfold it until the horse is calm and confident while standing underneath it.

Bridge
Your bridge can be made out of old pallets you pull apart and then nail together with the slats fitted closer together to offer a good walking surface. You can also use just a piece of plywood on the ground. The idea behind this is it's bigger than the pedestal offering a longer walking surface.

If you use a piece of plywood just be careful when it's wet as it can be slippery. To help with this I have added a welcome mat to the top of it. That is just another surface for your horse to become comfortable with!

Trotting Poles
Trotting poles can be old fence rails (with the nails removed), PVC pipes, fence posts, smooth tree branches, etc. Again, it's about using your imagination and digging up things that will give your horse something to think about. Using trotting poles is a great way to encourage your horse to look where he's going and be responsible for picking up his feet.

Trotting poles are also a great way to help strengthen stomach muscles and top lines. If you horse is out of shape and has a long, weak back, then you would start slow with the trotting rails, not expecting too much too soon. Just pepper them in throughout your training session.

Jumps
Again you can use anything lying around for jumps. PVC pipes, branches, line up some buckets lying on their sides, fence rails, or fence posts. Jumping helps your horse become more confident and less claustrophobic. Having your horse jump a few jumps will also help him become more athletic.

Cones/Buckets
You can set up some cones or buckets in a straight line for a weave pattern. Set up two cones for a figure of eight pattern. You can set them in a circle to help your horse stay out away from you.

I have also hidden treats under cones to encourage my horse to get creative and use his brain during a session. If my horse is acting closed off and grumpy, I will sometimes hide a few treats around my obstacle course to give him a purpose. Often times we have an idea in our head of what we want to accomplish, but it doesn't make sense to our horse. This is when the session will begin to feel like work instead of play, so it's alright to lighten things up a bit!

Instead of using the same obstacles for the same exercises all the time it's okay to mix things up. Instead of always jumping the jump, sometimes go up to it and then ask your horse to go sideways along it. You could weave in and out of the trotting poles instead of always trotting over them. These are just a few examples. Hopefully they have your creative juices flowing.

When you start with the obstacle course you can lead your horse through, if that's what he needs. Then, as you both build up some confidence, you can start moving back toward your horse's shoulder, then back to his hip, slowly making your way behind him. Whenever he loses confidence or gets confused just move back up to his head, support him through it, then go back behind him again. Don't sacrifice confidence to stay behind him in the driving zone. The horse's confidence is number one here.

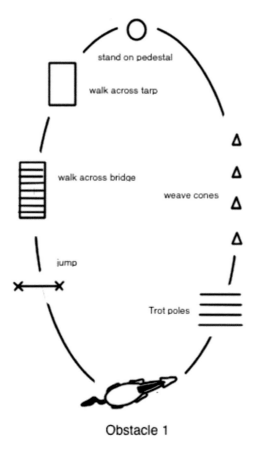
Obstacle 1

Step-By-Step Guide To Training A Miniature Horse To Drive

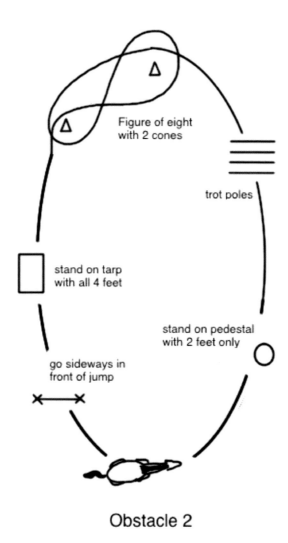

Obstacle 2

Step-By-Step Guide To Training A Miniature Horse To Drive

When you are both comfortable with the driving in halter and long lines, you can add the saddle part of the harness. This will also help you have a little more control over the lines, so they aren't looping down and getting under the horse's feet.

Once you have introduced the saddle and feel your horse is ready, it's time to hit the road for some more ground work miles!

Ground Driving

Here we have introduced the saddle, but continue to drive in the halter.

I ground drive all over my neighborhood. This gives the horse a chance to look around and see everything he will see when you start driving in cart. If he is curious about things, allow that curiosity. If something really worries your horse, allow him to stop and look. If he is really scared then you may want to retreat a bit, give him a chance to look again and then encourage him to go ahead and walk on by. This approach and retreat form of training will enhance your horse's confidence. It's not necessary to take a lot of time with each scary thing. Sometimes the appropriate response is to go ahead and just walk on by. This is where your focus will really help. If you are focused ahead, in the direction you want to go, and don't allow yourself to get all caught up with the scary cow, mail box, huge rock, barking dog, or neighbor horse, then your horse will likely follow your energy.

Once the horse is going well in the halter, knows whoa and can turn left and right well (without hesitation) it's time to introduce the bridle.

I use an open bridle, such as an English bridle, and let him wear it in his pen. Chewing a bit of hay, drinking water, just hanging out wearing the bridle without any demands made on him. This allows them to discover that the bit won't hurt them. I usually do chores while this is going on. I don't leave the horse unattended. I start with short periods of time, periodically through the day. Often by the second day, the horse has accepted the bit. Each horse is different, of course, and some may take a little longer than others.

The first one or two times I ground drive with the bit in the horses mouth I attach the driving lines to the halter rings. If I am using an English bridle I will put the halter over the top of the bridle. Once they are confidently moving forward and not worrying the bit, then I'll attach the driving lines to the bit. I do ground drive in an open bridle for some time and will even use an open bridle when I start using the travois.

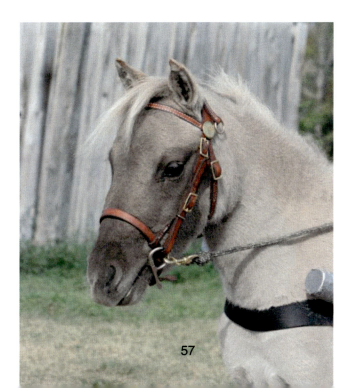

Chapter Five
The Travois

"In the steady gaze of the horse shines a silent eloquence that speaks of love and loyalty, strength and courage. It is the window that reveals to us how willing is his spirit, how generous his heart."
~Unknown

Once the horse is going confidently forward and knows all the commands you may enter the next step... the Travois! Many mini horse trainers choose to skip this step, because the mini is so easy to train. BUT I like to do every step, so I know they will be comfortable the whole way. Sometimes skipping steps can come back to haunt you!

I make my travois out of PVC pipe. I use two 10-foot lengths of 1-1/2" schedule 40 PVC pipe and connect the middle with a 4-foot, 3/4" schedule 40 piece of PVC. I wrap duct tape around the ends of the travois that are up by the horse's neck. They can be sharp and it's important to protect your horse.

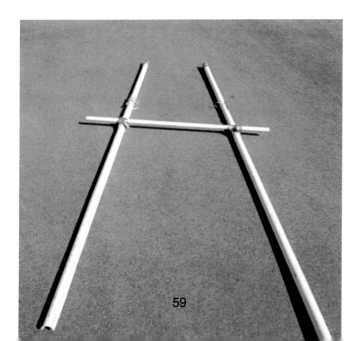

Step-By-Step Guide To Training A Miniature Horse To Drive

Make sure that your PVC will fit through your shaft loops and that it's long enough to drag on the ground, making some noise.

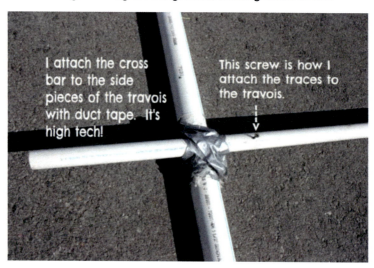

I start by dragging the travois around and allow the horse to follow it. This may take two people. Or you can drag it on one side of your body, while leading your horse on the other side, which seems to take the "scary" out of it.

When it's time to hook up the travois it's also time to harness on up! When harnessing make sure the harness is fitted properly. Be sure the harness you have fits your horse and isn't too big or too small. If the harness is too big it can really make things difficult for your horse, teaching them bad habits, such as putting their tongue over the bit. Also a badly fitting harness will sour a horse faster than anything else. This is very important!

If you plan on using one, the check should be fairly loose at first to let the horse get used to the idea. **Again if you are just learning, I recommend not using this piece of equipment.**

The breeching should cross the horse's rear, beneath the tail, about half way down, through the roundest part of the rear. The breeching ring should sit approximately level with the stifle, low enough it can't ride up under the tail and high enough it does not slip down into the hollow above the hind legs.

The saddle should be comfortable and not pressing into the horse's spine. It should sit about a hand's width back from the horse's shoulder, similar to where a riding saddle would sit. If the saddle does not have enough built-in padding to stay clear of the spine under pressure, you will need to add a pad to help distribute the weight.

You should be able to slide one finger between the crupper and the underside of the horse's tail. The back strap, which connects the saddle to the crupper, should be tight enough so the crupper doesn't flop around. The crupper shouldn't wiggle much when the horse moves, as this will cause rubbing (galling) under your horse's tail. It also shouldn't be so tight it pulls on the horse's tail, this will also make them sore. There is a fine line!

The bridle should fit comfortably as well. The horse's eye should be in the middle of the blinders. The noseband should be snug, it aids in keeping the horse's mouth shut so he can't get his tongue up over the bit. It should fit snug, but not so tight the horse is tossing his head and uncomfortable.

I don't like to have more than one wrinkle in the corner of the horse's mouth from the bit. I feel the corners of the horse's mouth and lips will fall asleep if the bit is too tight. Try holding the corners of your mouth tight enough to cause some wrinkles. Do your lips fall asleep? I learned this from an old cowboy. His horses always had such nice soft mouths. They were light and always ready for the next move. There wasn't any battle of wills because the horse was uncomfortable, or it's lips were asleep.

Once you are sure the harness is fitting correctly, then I go ahead and hook them up. I tighten the breeching up fairly snug to help control the travois. The breeching will keep the travois from swinging around too much, which can cause the tips of the "shafts" to dig into the horse's neck when turning.

If you feel your horse needs the support you can lead them, at their head, for a few steps and through a couple of turns, until they can navigate by themselves. Or if you have a helper, have them be up at the horse's head while you are driving from behind.

I have them go up and down hills. Make sure that you have the breeching snug up around their rear so they know what it will feel like. That way when you drive them down a hill and the breeching tightens, holding the cart off the horse, they won't get scared.

Hitching the Travois to the Horse

First lead your horse into the travois.

Step-By-Step Guide To Training A Miniature Horse To Drive

And ready to hitch!

First you will lift the travois up and run the "shafts" through the shaft loops. Then attach the traces to the cross bar of the travois.

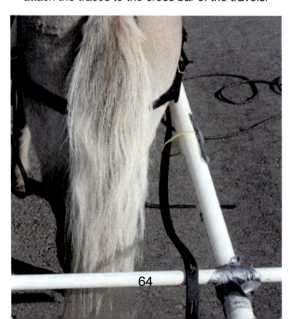

Step-By-Step Guide To Training A Miniature Horse To Drive

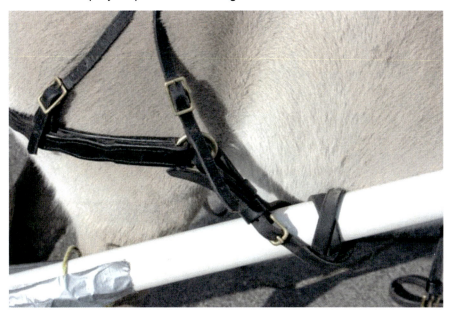

Above: Right side of horse.

Next wrap the breeching straps around the "shafts" of the travois.

Below: Left side of horse.

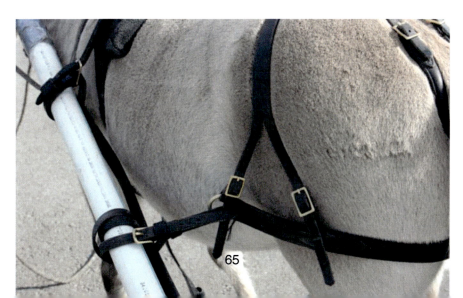

Step-By-Step Guide To Training A Miniature Horse To Drive

Photo Left: Then you will wrap your wrap straps in a Figure Eight, around the "shafts" of the travois, keeping the travois close to the horse's sides. See page 79 for instructions on the Figure Eight Wrap.

All done and ready to drive away!

You can either drive them in the halter or move on to the bridle at this step. I prefer to start them in the open bridle here, so they are fully aware of what is going on behind them.

I drive them in the arena, out on the driveway, and down our neighborhood roads, both the gravel and paved roads in the travois, before I drive them in the cart. Then they can learn how it feels to spook between shafts and how to handle the restriction on their sideways movement without fear. Ask them to walk, trot and even canter while driving in the travois. That way they will learn how it feels in all the different gaits. It's important that they are familiar with all movement that way if they spook and take off a little bit, they aren't scared more by the way the travois feels when they are cantering.

The travois also sounds different on the pavement than it does on the gravel and grass. So it's a good idea to introduce them to all the different surfaces. The cart will not be as noisy as the travois is! Do this until your horse is comfortable, is confidently moving forward and you feel it's ready to move to the next step: hitching to the cart.

Step-By-Step Guide To Training A Miniature Horse To Drive

Step-By-Step Guide To Training A Miniature Horse To Drive

Chapter Six
Hitching the Cart

"Your horse can only be as brave as you are."
~Pat Parelli

Now it's time to hitch your horse to your cart! A very exciting step. It's a good idea to do this with a friend around. It just helps calm everyone's nerves to have some support.

I tie the horse for the harnessing. After the horse is harnessed I put the bridle on and lead the horse to the vehicle.

I lead the horse around to the front of the cart, while the cart is tipped up with the shafts pointing up in the air. I reach up with one hand, grab the shafts, and bring them down over the horse. It does help if you have someone to hold the horse for you while you do this step. If you don't have a helper it is possible to do this alone. Especially if your horse has had all the ground work done. They should be standing quietly for you by this time.

Step-By-Step Guide To Training A Miniature Horse To Drive

When lowering the shafts down over the horse, put your foot in front of the wheel of the cart so it won't roll forward into your horse as you get it adjusted.

Push the shafts through the tugs and attach the traces to the cart first. If the horse moves suddenly the cart won't fall out of the tugs and frighten him. Attach the traces to the single tree on the cart.

Then do up the breeching, so if the horse tries to back up, he will not bang into the cart with his rear or hocks, scaring him. Do up the wrap straps last. The wrap straps are only needed when there is someone in the cart. They help hold the shafts down in the tugs.

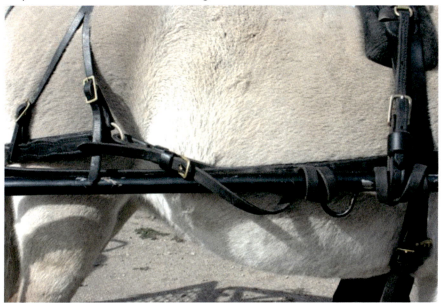

This photo shows how to wrap the breeching wrap straps around the shaft.

Note: catching the trace in the breeching wrap. This helps the traces stay where they belong and not sag down.

This is how I wrap the wrap straps around the shafts in the Figure Eight style. It is important to wrap these snuggly, not too tight and not too loose. This will help balance the cart. You don't want it so tight there is constant pressure on the horse's belly and you don't want it so loose the shafts bounce up and down putting pressure on the horse's back. There is a fine line, a balance point.

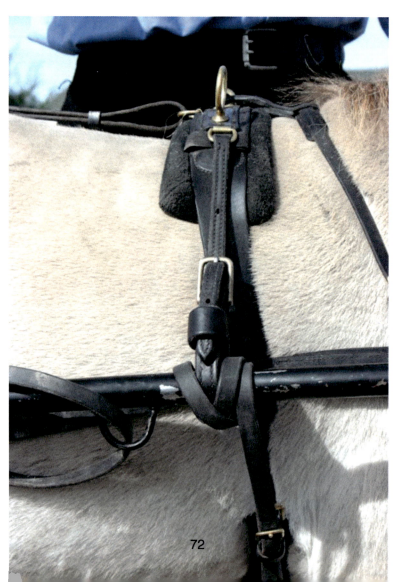

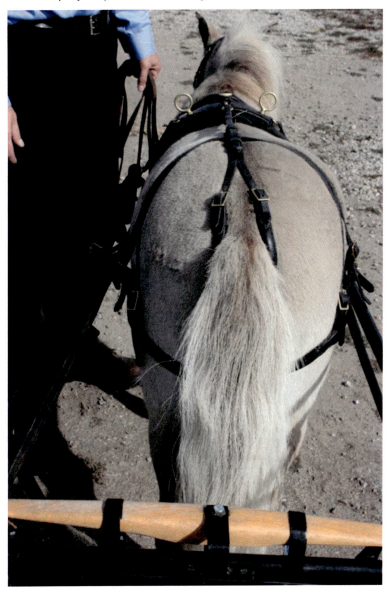

Finally, the view from the cart!

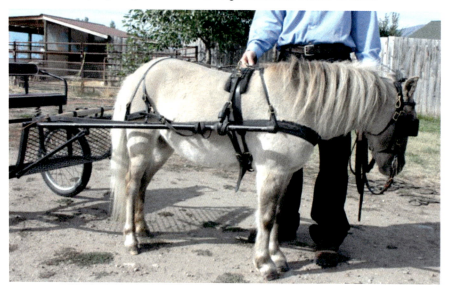

Properly harnessed and ready to go.

Before you hop in and drive off be sure you check the balance of the cart. It should look like it is going slightly uphill from the seat to the horse. Put your hand under the saddle to feel how much weight is resting on the horse's back. If you have the cart balanced correctly, once you are sitting in the seat, there should be no weight resting on the horse's back.

The above photo shows an unbalanced cart. It's just a little bit off, but would be enough to make the horse uncomfortable. It's the little details that matter in horsemanship.

In this photo the cart is adjusted correctly and well balanced. I simply adjusted the shaft loops by shortening them up a hole to bring the shafts up more, giving the whole set up an uphill look.

For the first couple yards it's okay to follow along behind the cart and not climb right in. That way you can see how the horse is going to handle the cart. It's also a good idea to have a helper here, to help steady the horse. Really though, if you aren't rushing your horse, and he has successfully pulled the travois for awhile, this step will be fairly easy for him.

I don't dilly dally behind the cart for very long. I like to trot!

Once you are settled on the seat watch the horse for any signs of him being uncomfortable. Have someone put their hand under the saddle to test the weight on the horse's back since there is now someone in the cart.

Step-By-Step Guide To Training A Miniature Horse To Drive

Here is a little photo lesson on proper rein position. If you hold them this way it will make it easier to hold the whip as well.

The pinky finger points toward the horse and the ends of the reins go up and forward, between the thumb and the pointer finger. Thumbs point up toward the sky.

Here is a bigger shot of how to hold the reins and the whip. Be sure you don't allow the long ends of the reins to fall down below the floor or drag on the road as you drive. Be careful they don't tangle around your feet either. I usually just loop the end of the reins around one of my pinkies to keep it gathered up.

Step-By-Step Guide To Training A Miniature Horse To Drive

Off you go! Just be aware of your surroundings. Be watchful, but not waiting for the worst. As in riding, watch where you are going. They can feel that, and will go the direction you are looking, most of the time. If you have done all the steps correctly and the horse is comfortable in his harness and cart, he will really enjoy driving with you. They like to be useful and they also enjoy seeing the neighborhood!

It's important to remember it takes lots of practice and time to make a great driving horse. Your horse will only be better the more thoroughly he understands each step, so take your time and don't rush yourselves.

A horse will be a happy driving companion the more comfortable he is in his work. So be very sure his harness and cart fit him and his needs. Be flexible as the needs can change over time. And always be open minded to learning new things. It seems there is always more to learn and more than enough people out there willing to help!

Driving can be a very rewarding experience to share with your horse, so take your time and enjoy each step! I promise it will pay off in the end.

Figure Eight Wrap

Figure 1: Shows the wrap strap coming from below, in front of the shaft loop and shaft to be wrapped around the shaft.

Figure 2: Shows the wrap strap crossing behind the shaft loop then wrapping around the shaft.

Figure 3: Shows how I then bring the wrap strap behind the shaft and the shaft loop to wrap it around the front of the shaft.

Figure 4: Shows the strap then going back down to be buckled up snuggly.

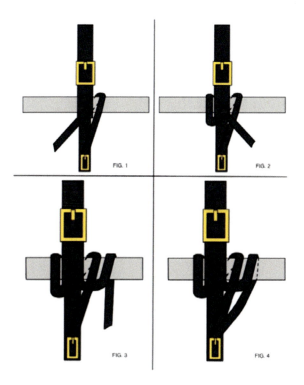

Books I Love

Carriage Driving, A Logical Approach Through Dressage Training
    Heike Bean and Sarah Blanchard

Harnessing Up
    Anne Norris and Caroline Douglas

Driving Questions Answered
    Sallie Walrond

Schooling Horses in Hand
    Richard Hinrichs

What Horses Say, How to Hear, Help and Heal Them
    Anna Clemence Mews and Julie Dicker

Spoken In Whispers, The Autobiography of a Horse Whisperer
    Nicci MacKay

The Power of Positive Horse Training, Saying Yes to Your Horse
    Sarah Blanchard

Zen Horse, Zen Mind
    Allan J. Hamilton

The Tao of Eqqus
    Linda Kohanov

About the Author

Mindy Schroder has been blessed with horses her whole life. From growing up on the back of her Shetland Ponies, to getting her first "big" horse when she was 10 years old, horses have been the central point of her life.

It was after she became a mother that miniature horses waltzed into her life. For seven years she raised, trained and showed miniature horses. Mostly she trained for other people and gave driving lessons on the farm. It was because of this experience, she discovered a need for a simple "how-to" manual for the every day horse person.

And The Step-By-Step Guide To Training A Miniature Horse To Drive was born!

Made in the USA
Monee, IL
19 March 2024